The Van Gogh Notebook

THE VAN GOGH NOTEBOOK

Peter Cooley

Carnegie Mellon University Press

Pittsburgh 2004

For Joshua

Acknowledgments

Grateful acknowledgment is made to the editors of the magazines in which the following poems appeared:

The Chariton Review: "Meadow with Butterflies," "The Woman at Café Tambourin."
The Georgia Review: "The Potato Eaters."
Interim: "Pavement Café at Night" ("Shall I write a poem . . .")
The Louisville Review: "Self-Portrait as Van Gogh," "The Chair and Pipe," "The Starry Night," "Road with Cypresses," "Wheatfield Under a Threatening Sky with Crows."
Northeast: "Sunflowers," "Olive Orchard," "The Last Self-Portrait."
Ploughshares: "Tarascon Diligence."
Prairie Schooner: "Garden of the Hospital at Arles," "Olive Trees in a Mountain Landscape," "Orchard Bordered by Cypresses."
Quarterly West: "Orchard with Peach Blossom."
Raccoon: "The Enclosed Field," "Portrait of Dr. Gachet," "Le Mousmé."
The Sewanee Review: "Harvest Landscape: Blue Cart," "The Iron Bridge at Trinquetaille."
The Sonora Review: "Still Life, Hat and Pipe," "Public Garden at Arles," "Gauguin's Chair."
The Southern Review: "Landscape with Ploughed Fields," "Undergrowth with Two Figures," "The Bedroom at Arles."
The Southern Poetry Review: "Self-Portrait."
Tar River Poetry: "Self-Portrait in Front of an Easel," "A Wheat Field."
Three Rivers Poetry Journal: "The Loom," "Still Life with Open Bible," "Pietà."
The Virginia Quarterly Review: "Fishing Boats on the Beach at Saintes-Maries," "Stairway at Auvers," "Self-Portrait with Soft Felt Hat."

I wish to thank Tulane University Graduate School for two summer grants which allowed for the writing of poems and the preparation of this manuscript. I am grateful to my wife Jacki and to Richard Katrovas for advice and criticism of this book as it took shape. To Rosemary Eddins particular thanks are due for her assistance.

Library of Congress Control Number: 2003103709
ISBN 0-88748-411-5
Copyright © 1987 by Peter Cooley
All rights reserved
Printed and bound in the United States of America
First Carnegie Mellon University Press
Classic Contemporaries Edition, 2004

10 9 8 7 6 5 4 3 2 1

The publisher would like to express his gratitude to James Reiss and James W. Hall for their assistance in producing this volume.

Contents

I

THE LOOM

Unless light be applied to it like a poultice
sex will not heal in us.
It is a wound less scabrous than any.
Therefore, invisible, Vincent set down here
the landlady's daughter, then the widow, then the whore,
within this little gnome upright over a thread
and composed the man in himself he must have lost
to lust for three women in succession hopelessly.
Or did he sit his ghost inside this frame
and spin out Margot who threatened death after he fled?
Whatever, the facts wash off in this clear air,
reduced to a clean Dutch radiance
which sets all things at such rigid angles to each other
they assume the attitude of prayer.
Kneel down, little weaver, in the falling light,
your heart is a bobbin, it cannot stop
thrashing and trembling even if the shuttle stop.
The loom is a cage. Our bodies are another.
The light falls, a man and woman trade their threads in it.
The light fails and they stumble, fall in it.
They move through each other, they touch and separate.
They find themselves raveled in the expanse of a great cloth.

THE POTATO EATERS

Not ever to sit down, a part of one another
in the old way this hunger takes for granted—
this is how we stand, the woman thinks.

Not ever to be apart from one another
the man thinks, at the altar of the table,
the potatoes almost weightless on our tongues.

And the tea—let me speak—in thick, bone mugs
consuming them entirely until, risen,
their spirits can be thanksgiving's scrawny ghost.

Without him, she tastes this to herself, shakes on more salt.
Without her, he savors it, with other women.
And the bastings, *might, could,* seal in the precious juice.

They prepare a feast at the table of each other.
They sit down, bowed in silence, tooth and claw
ruddy at the unspoken, ravening.

STILL LIFE WITH OPEN BIBLE

Our fathers die for us just once.
Thereafter, no one to stand up for him
a man is already on his feet
at the first whisper of the given name.
Who has left this great book open?
The pages, mottled dun and pink,
run together, unreadable, the binding broken.
All night it has been raining in Nuenen.
The candles beside the tome have long been snuffed
by the lamentations of the sky,
the wailing which must have touched this newspaper
sodden before the book. Look,
immersed, it has emerged
just like the scripture demanding that we read it
when like the other it cannot keep its word.

A WHEAT FIELD

If happiness is this, a field of wind
through which the stubble, wheat and sky
pass on whatever journey, rinsed by the sun,
then, yes, I have had my time with it.
Or if that word is a single meadowlark
fixed to the clouds, the clouds that cannot cease
shifting their weather whenever and continuing.

However the wind goes, it is only radiance.

There is an absence of all shadow
wherever I go here and whenever
the light follows or I follow it. However—

STILL LIFE, HAT AND PIPE

Otherwise, the body, too, could not be satisfied
nor the mind's eye blinded by such dark.
The bottle, pot, the basket, pipe and hat
compose as music will, by losses, remembered touch.
Vincent, you read in Dickens of the fire
which drawn on would smoke the demons out,
the shrieking ones who surround themselves with flame
to bear us upward till we scale banked clouds' rarest air.

Still, the pipe insists on reeling me, my no-no-no,
against a black ground, swarming.
Crazy or not, here I come, nightfall,
with some words I write on vertigo:
let me bare my head, wear my trembling, ragged breath
so light that the clouds can draw it up
when I go out this minute to take in stars.

SELF-PORTRAIT IN FRONT OF AN EASEL

Back to us, the easel's picture must burn blue,
bituminous to cast this smoky pitch
over the suffering blazoned in Vincent's flesh.
Who burns there? He stares straight into it.

Blue his cheekbones, the brow's receding flush,
the flames combed back over the fire inside.
Blue his jacket, the palette, brushes in his clutch
and bluest the eyes in which the other picture hides.

How to decode this? To signify the sign
for those lines around the eyes, a mirror of the mirror
in the unseen where the seer, seeing, is seen?
Suppose I told you the face was my own there,
would you keep reading? Would you continue
if I said he was anyone but you?

THE WOMAN AT CAFÉ TAMBOURIN

Women, listen. You and I know
a woman is a wound, healing to bleed.

Some of you take in a man, suffer him stiffly.
By these means men declare their passion,

erect ceremonies of the hearth and child
so history is assured its repetition.

Not so with me. I sleep with anyone
who lingers to help me close up my café.

But for my suffering I go to those with demons
that I may seek my twin and put to sleep

the death rattle of this drum inside my head
for which I named the café I labor in—

as if my business were an exorcism!
The patrons shout, "Belle Agostina, be my wife,"

too dumb to know Agostina never weds
having seen what sleeps in most,

all their lusts lapdogs against mine.
Ah, but the possessed ones, painters all,

they don't propose, though I have framed their demons
and my patrons sit beneath these torments, drunken.

Painters lust like me. And one especial,
Vincent, too much he drew my soul

into his breath which named the world
the colors earth had never seen.

15

Too *intime,* we were too *intime.* I spurned him,
filling my womb with a fool's child

bled to a chemist in a backstreet.
Women, you understand. In this portrait my dress

like everything about me is pretense
which Vincent could see through at a glance

and repeated my scarlet hat in scarlet bands
around my scarlet table, beer stein, cigarette.

He knew too much, that one, of jubilation
we women suffering insist on if we speak.

16

SELF-PORTRAIT WITH SOFT FELT HAT

You who would die into some other,
allow these colors of the sea and sky
to take you in. Fins, wings. The elements are free.
Released, you have only to immerse yourself.
Blue cradles you, now you are born aloft, afloat,
passing into the dreamscape of this face
approaching calm. Cobalt, azure, sapphire:
there is nowhere Vincent has not lost himself
in strokes whirling the background up to his body's edge
and now across it: jacket, tie, hat,
and red beard blued, the cheeks, the brow, the eyes
blue bluing blue. In this gaze you may rest and enter.
These eyes have taken down the stars, walked corridors along the deep
searching for you. Turquoise, lapis. Sleep. Sleep.

MONTMARTRE

In the great myth that we begin life over
each new place we move to, the sky supports us,
accepting the perspective drawn by fog,
restoring the numinous to all things.
Vincent saw this. Paris had no color
nor did Montmartre he hadn't seen before.
His first immersion here in the Impressionists
bathed the hill gray; he baptized fence and tree,
lamppost, a balcony, five figures,
Vincent, Vincent's gray; his faceless face washed up on itself.
The hill was not a skull; it couldn't think.
He set his cross up, cross-hatched in post and bough
as his easel set him up. Color was all.
After two years he fled, resurrected all at Arles.

II

THE ORCHARD

If I could lose myself in light
it might be like this: the man, the woman,
their bodies blossoming beside the trees,
these apple boughs whose petals correspond.
It might be springtime, they are singing some sweet nothing.
She might extend her arms where the limbs meet
in their extensions skyward and pluck some lush, white thing
as invitation. And then he draws her down
across the ground until the ground swells with them
years thereafter. No, it cannot happen like that.
But there are trees like Vincent's to set us dreaming.
And, imagined, a white whiter than the memory of any body.

ORCHARD WITH PEACH BLOSSOM

Between earth and heaven a south wind lights on the peach trees.
Their branches begin a chorus, lavender answers the pink.
The horizon draws down, cypresses play green rime
on the foreground: earth, adance, shakes out its own.
Nothing human distracts the first flowering
but a fence running gold through the center,
a reminder some man crossed this way once
and impatient to make something happen
passed on. As even the sun now
which arranged the scene, makes it happen.
And a thousand years from now
or until someone's eyes leave this page
which is not a page but a canvas,
which is not itself but an image, Vincent,
will watch the same wind take it down.

HARVEST LANDSCAPE: BLUE CART

Azure, the cart, dead center,
burns bluer than the sky, clearer,
more self-consuming in its essential hue.
The hay is in. A lone stack at the left
reflects the noon like the gold dome of a mosque
as if in wait for some priest or bedlamite
to straddle upward chanting thanks to God.
The hay is in. The plains compose themselves
from foreground to horizon, umber, copper, bronze
in gradations of completion approaching gold.
While blue mottled hills await
above the barns' squat orange roofs
the rake, the hay, the long days of the baling.
So many lifetimes they have watched it come to pass,
these elevations which ask nothing of the plain,
a process of the human, a despoilment,
the blue cart has been freed from for today.
This noon it burns like them on the sun's reflected flame
detached from any craft or beauty, ravishing
without which we who plunder could not sustain us.

THE SOWER

After the resurrection, we, the chosen, will arise
and the earth plowed violet, the sun's fecund yellow blood,
will release an evening like this one for our birth.
The fields will have opened in the swelling of their tombs
golden and mauve, the sweet fetor of the loam
will walk the sillions with us, a spring beneath our foot
which is the sky's reflection, the last extension of its reach.
How lightly we will step out of our tombs at twilight here
after eons of sleep, swinging our new limbs to the wind
and watch as our fist opens its seeds and crows descend
and the crows arising will be our chosen friends.
Here in the afterlife, our sun can never set.
It can stop the night, it is one moment before dusk.
Glory swoops down to squat and shake its hungry maw.
It, too, is gold along its claw and ragged wings.
We are the suicides, risen in a body
knowing no world but that which expectation makes
of wind or bird or earth on which we work,
here at the end of time, our sowing a ceaseless sport.
And darkness, from which seeds might lift their heads to stalks and chaff,
never descends to grace this light, unmerciless, the stench
releasing its rank flood over oblivion.

FISHING BOATS ON THE BEACH AT SAINTES-MARIES

Half the eye is heaven here. You could look for Vincent in it
clouded in lavender or white, pearled, iridescent.
But his desire was to line the earth with color,
to draw the rainbow down along the ground.
So we descend: the boats float on the golden beach,
prows, riggings and masts in a cat's cradle
bent seaward. While the sand beneath them undulates
the sterns toss forward, lumbering, luminous,
continuing their still course, landlocked, always sailing.
And in response the water stands at our attention
on which the boats at sea, unmoving, pitch, fishing.
The shores' boats hold the sea in place
that the fish may swim up, dazzling in their nets,
these pearly nets beneath a patch of turquoise, out of the picture.
Land, sea, which fishes most? Ask the wind, yourself, trafficking
    between them.

29

OLD PEASANT (PATIENCE ESCALIER)

Better to watch your flesh wither or to desert it?
This is the conundrum of old age.
And the subject in question leaves no answer.
Behind him the sky is falling always
between gold and orange, a nimbus angelless
while his cape, the matchlight azure of a saint,
brushes up the eternal. Or has it skirted back
to walk over his body and the three good legs,
that staggering answer to the fabled riddle?

His hat, no protection from the sun of Arles,
weighs on the brow, a crown bearing him down
where the features, that veil on which like Christ
Vincent impressed his own, baffle us most.
Beatific? Resigned? The eyes shift every time
we return to choose taking them on.
Vincent must have known. That shifting is the age he never got to.

THE POSTMAN ROULIN

Drunk, drunk, drunk. That's how he came to me
and like a lad, that Vincent, but not much drunk on wine,
more on a wheatstalk or every fortnight, maybe, a whore,

a choice Arlésienne you buy to root up like a hog
or suck. Me, don't I know, who's got the itch
even holy days while Mama rocks one of our brood,

then stumbling home, begging for more, pardieu!
After, I'm still pricking and say my rosary
just to come down. The bottle, too,

she's just another bitch between my lips:
once I'm high I'm flying to get off—
Holy Mother, I always end up on the floor.

Vincent? Shit, he'd get a little stinking,
him, on one absinthe and then, delirious,
he'd be reeling, setting up his easel,

chewing paints Theo had mailed him—
they were his soup, that pipe his entrée, cheese and fruit.
He squandered more on tobacco than food, fucking or booze.

(One swore to me in bed that ear he cut was dole,
the cheapskate! Not that he owed her much,
shouldn't I know, who caught him myself

sneaking home, him standing in the field,
candles in his hat to paint the stars.)
He was immortal, I loved him, the bastard.

No, like I say, he was a lad,
a prodigal, what do you say, a prodigy,
my own but out of me such light could never come.

Look you, how nicely he's posed me as I speak
like a proper postman, the word "Postes" on my hat,
my eight brass buttons, the gold braid on my sleeve

matching my beard. The artist matches, I know that.
I love the bastard. He was a prodigy, look at me.
This one is good. Immortal. Look at me.

SUNFLOWERS

That you be nothing but the light, but its arrangement.

* * *

That you seize the buds of noon, offer up your own gold blood.
That you be the bee, a beast more holy than the host.
That you buzz, glut, that you hum, hummmm.

* * *

That you swing, drunk, never having drunk.
That you shine, light on light.
That you step out, that you cakewalk: hey, man! that you tango, fandango.

* * *

That you pan air, bear away the sift of silt.
That you glint, gold leaf, gold petal, gold disc, stems.

* * *

That you sound the gold chords, diminishing, repeating.
And sound the music while it perishes.

* * *

And succeed yourself, yourselves, all crowns.

* * *

And therefore to be touched but to dance, sound of limb.

* * *

That you elect yourself a trophy of the sun.

NIGHT CAFÉ

Mortals, this is the legend of the stars. Listen while one speaks.
When Van Gogh drew us inside for conspiring with man
we were banished to the spasms of these four lamps.
Caged, we spluttered bile on furniture and floor;
the billiard table, bar, the chairs and tables, furious
swam against each other, yellowed in our wrath.
But it was green and red, the ceiling and the walls,
the master said could house homeless imbibers,
heads bowed to their drained glasses. One figure, standing watch,
    took them all in:
the room too deep for their diminished stare,
those eyes, almost extinguished, never catching him.
Like a doctor or a priest, the garçon, dressed in white,
steps out, Vincent, as you assumed, choosing this night
to refuse himself that tippling he has denied us.

PUBLIC GARDEN AT ARLES

I'm not sure how to say this.
Sometimes, as now, stepping through the frame
I am a woman. Lost in her black dress,
my body hers, a dress within a dress,
my breath divides and half fills, female.
Then the man beside me, me in ochre hat,
grasps my hand, his. All mere complexities
burn off in noon's blue heat and rise,
steeping their evening where shadows of the pine,
protector and provider, yield,
enter, withdraw, releasing their green balm.
The resin, stinging, strips our lips and eyes.
And afterward, the couple processes down some blind white path.
Vincent, you divined the scene, you arranged the rendezvous.
You tell me I am more the man confessing it.

PAVEMENT CAFÉ AT NIGHT

What choice is there but joy?
She looks through him, repeating it,
this woman, seated with her man
before the table's clarifying white,
the two one shadow almost
burnished with a Van Gogh radiance
set along the canopy's full length,
burning on itself, gold, luminescent.
They are lost here among couples like themselves
bedecking a scene whose narrow street,
the cobblestones and steeple, washed with midnight,
all things caught on a deep blue undertow,
is over-picturesque and tedious,
flecked with too much expectation of the obvious.
They might like lovers at either hand
be bored were it not for the canopy
lit by a single gaslight
the others have dismissed as ordinary,
too tiny to shed magnificence.
Joy, what's that, the man asks,
when he would like to weep before such grace,
such singling out, that they should wait,
extending their gold instants as they spend them.
Yet he skirts, like her, with a question,
a sentence neither of them answers.
And the night sky, its canopy of stars,
wheels over them and Fortune, yawning,
elects to sport with Time
in someone else's bed but marks their names
for tomorrow, maybe, sparing them Her eyeless gaze
that they may spend themselves all night,
two prodigals their language yokes in separation.

PAVEMENT CAFÉ AT NIGHT

"Shall I write a poem," the husband whispered to his wife,
"and put us in it, a poem after Van Gogh,
where you could see yourself, reflected, beautifully?"
"Do it or don't," the woman answered at the verge of sleep.
She lay beneath him, weary of his appeasements.
Soon the poem appeared, naked at the window,
speechless, manic as the man and in full color,
demanding to be written down. Our poet rolled over and began:
I sit with my wife outdoors at a café
facing a cobblestone square. Behind us other couples
process a street down which a carriage, horse-drawn,
shortly will emerge, and at tables all around
the even more devoted wait for dawn
they will discover in one another's eyes.
Scintillant, the night sky reels over fireworks of stars
to saturate our thirst for any golder gold—
oh, it is all too exquisite to be put down . . .
The poet drifted, mooning above his still white sheet
on which he hoped to pen, in tribute to his wife.
He stared into the poem: an incandescence spoke:
"Poet, what is this awning a single gas lamp lit
above the lovers' heads like a canopy of fire
golder than manuscripts the sacred walks out of?
Poet, turn to your wife, read the next line and the next
in her stuporous breath. The fire stands above you
as if the present were consumed and your gold face,
hers, too, were interchangeable and featureless.
This is what it is to be content. Write me down, singing,
rubbing your eyes, aching, anxious to be done."
The husband trembled, the words jerked from his hand:
We sit at the café. The night is always lifting.
And the stars above us reflect a corresponding gold
as morning puts them out, light extinguishing light
or feeding it, in imitation of the human . . .

SELF-PORTRAIT

A saint, a hermit, might shave his head and beard
this close to blood, memento mori of the skull.
But only you, against a ground robin's egg blue,
would dare to number the red hairs growing back.
Starveling, your face has gnawn on wind,
the gristle of the mistral, panted all night
to draw from summer's end the high yellow note
higher. The sound tasted like ash, resounding.
Famished, you painted it all over, out of earshot
in your melodious blue. You knew it was a music impermissible
except to the most human. Here you invite us now to feast
on the real meat of your features, the geometry of hunger.
And yet you set that robin's egg within each eye.
Eyes the tawny red of beard and hair . . .

PUBLIC GARDEN WITH WEEPING TREE:
POET'S GARDEN I

There is a willow I planted in my yard
to weep for me those minutes before rain,
minutes the sky dyes saffron, dies out green.
And there is another, invisible, within myself
I will never see but must send prayers to
no matter what the weather. Neither cries enough.
And so around my tears a garden must be raised,
the boughs protected by a bower, the soul a body.
In my next life I will know a painter's life
and return to the flesh Vincent cast off
to walk these shadows some afternoon in Arles.
I will be walking toward the whores nearby. It will be 1888
or 2038. Vincent will be busy with this life,
teaching himself to cry in this morning's summer shower.

IRON BRIDGE AT TRINQUETAILLE

Here iron calls to iron, stone to stone,
concrete to the morning smelted blue
by some rare element in the light itself
which makes of its arrival a descent.

Blue, a flying buttress spanning the upper left,
the bridge suspends its little figures in a cage.
And on the right through a crypt-blue viaduct,
the cobblestones release two wanderers into space.

Between them, dead center, countless in blue cement,
the steps proceed in perpetual rise and fall.
Yet all the figures except one are in ascent
and she, char-black, a saint cut from the stake,

looms pregnant in a billowing black gown.
She occupies no special step, she floats
as if the way upward and downward are the same
until across her shoulders the scarlet gashes cease to run.

Here she bled deepest after the blazes died
and she cut herself down from the wooden cross of love.
Now she is released. Free to wander, aimless,
to travel the stairs on her bare knees, to be caged.

This is desire's aftermath in Van Gogh's legend.

TARASCON DILIGENCE

Today the world will be enough.
You will devote yourself to the six essential colors,
balancing the motion of these wheels
the two coaches lock in place. Face to face,
one red-paneled, one green-coifed
foreground, background, they wait together
holding down the violet earth
yawning beneath them, the shadows of abyss.
And the sky, a single blue wedge
tacked up in the right corner, must suffice
to free you by its unmitigated hue,
its failure to share the trappings of either coach.
Before the gold wall, however, a brown ladder
propped against the carriage to the left
assures us that rising, if only to the top,
is still in order. Follow me up the dull rungs.
You may ascend to the empty seat and take the air,
suspension being everything. Here, to stay put, to keep
one foot separate from the other in such ether
is work enough. Or for a moral:
requires wings you drew in on the ground.

THE BEDROOM AT ARLES

There is one solitude
more essential than the others:
the throat aches, desiring speech,
the hand, nothing before it,
grapples with air to measure this
and draw the color from such weight and music.
From these burdens a man may find himself
released suddenly into his body
which is song, no longer his.
So, friend, again tonight the walls are down:
I step, wary, into your nervous kingdom.
This is the room you have left me
where poems come from, in some fragile, clear response.
I try one chair, then the other.
I perch on the bed's red coverlet.
Silence becomes me, doesn't it?
A prayer: let me wait this out
with your help given time.
The poems of the other life have all been written
here, before I began.
I have only to hesitate, to refuse to speak.
Later, everything you whisper I will appreciate;
and later still will master;
and later still on this white canvas will write down.

PORTRAIT OF ARMAND ROULIN

I

Once a boy-man in a black porkpie,
black jacket, white shirt, white cravat
against a ripe green backdrop. Once, beyond description
the poem in him. Once, these eyes fixed out of the picture
on secrets drawing down a mouth
about his throat, where, unresolved,
the voice which has no language swells in speech.
What might squeak out if he released it once?
We who have known the quiet of sons
being sons, taken for sullenness,
which becomes the silence of men
and is thought stubbornness, or, given time,
authority or wisdom, will not intrude.
Armand Roulin, the postman's son,
at seventeen no boy cries out to hear himself
sound less than himself. The portrait is the least of all your poses.

II

Now you tell us you have become a man
in three months' time. I nod, I nod.
Squarely your shoulders prop a center up
on which your jacket, flooded with the noon sun,
props you up. Undone, your collar and black cravat
set off the porkpie at its waggish tilt.
Your beard, thickening across the upper lip,
attempts a fine mat to distract us from your mouth,
winsome and bowed as any virgin's pout.
Of course, the eyes, which you are blind to,
of necessity permit no such disguises,
their hazel depths receding upon the whites,
having seen the dead center through Vincent's own
and knowing, unlike him, they find no images to refract them.

L'ARLÉSIENNE: MADAME GINOUX

Nothing can staunch it, this light within his eyes
racing to catch her, light the odor of his death
and so Madame stares past Vincent, to herself naked.

She recalls herself Mademoiselle, in her first beauty
half a life ago: how the calyx of her sex
yearned to be unfolded; how she ran, aching

in her summer cottons, billowing,
that her flesh be touched by the mistral
at bodice and at crotch; how she unloosed

from her sepals the perfume like ripe camellias
until she divided from their throng
the young men, throbbing, one by one,

how she drew them to her, sapped them,
how she dragged them down her till they dropped.
So long ago . . . What might have drawn her,

she wonders, to this man, laying her down
like a Japanese: black gown, black hair,
black ribbons, he has cut her out,

a silhouette against a bitter yellow ground.
Now he flattens her face, drains it of blood
like a Kabuki mask, the flesh beneath it male.

He knows too much, she thinks, and dresses it
as me, as any woman, of the woman in himself
and has slept with that body as himself

sleeping alone, sleeping with any woman.
Small wonder the death mask hurts my eyes
looking into his, small wonder he still lives
this sexlessness in which my sex disappears
with him dead center. Small wonder all my life
I never wanted one this deep.

LE MOUSMÉ

Now I am fourteen I am old enough
Mama says—as if I needed her permission!—
to pose alone with this stranger for an hour,

a week of hours, if peering at me, nose on mine
while he paints, Mama says, is all he asks.
Monsieur Vincent isn't *beau*. His eyes

burn red like the sun at dawn,
the sun at dusk, red like my dress
and his beard flames orange and bizarre.

Mama says he is a gentleman
from Paris and the North Countries,
he was a minister, his father, too,

so he's cultured like us, the Japanese,
and we're all *étrangers* in Arles.
As if I didn't know it, me the only Japonnaise

at school, no one to court me ever!
She says if he's drunk in his yellow house
with that dashing Monsieur Gauguin who passes me

smiling on the street or visits the bad women
we should forgive him. Mama says look down
when those women dressed in black go by,

down, down, so I look up: crimson stockings, faces
scarved, black dresses at noon, gold spiked heels,
ankle bracelets every one, perfume like apples we've let fall!

(I wonder if they're Japanese under their scarves?)
If I could strut out like one of them I'd run away,
to Paris maybe, wouldn't Mama be sorry

and have to cry like I'd been ruined? I wonder . . .
does she think this picture will be proper for our parlor
so the old Arlésiennes can be invited over?

Gads, wait till she sees it. My skirt all dots
on the canvas, my blouse all stripes. Together!
And I wore solid red here to look at least eighteen!

But Monsieur Proper drew my face puffed up like Mama's.
Merde! I look more like my mama's mama than Mama!
To be painted by a redbearded minister of Mama's

when all I dream every night is to strut out,
one of the black silk ladies, and not be hung up here
with North Country foreigners and redheads

or not sit in parlors looking some picture of Mama
but instead to go down to that yellow house
and flash my white teeth in the dark to Paul Gauguin!

THE CHAIR AND PIPE

Because on earth the stars have counterparts
always we must go on standing here
appointed to this duty without being asked.
Therefore, the four legs joined to one another
by a seat which refuses to sit still
keep up their dancing even as we wait.
It looks like this: the red tiles of the floor,
running to some other measure, are a roof
and the chair is set with the extinguished pipe,
above it, on it, about to take the sky.
It will not take the sky.
                              The chair is gold,
waxed so fine no words could hold it now.
These words of which the chair is first a shadow
and the shadow some color Vincent threw down
to show he walked the stars. He never walked.
And the stars, too, are literal, they appear
as they did to me last night
looking like nothing so I might give them lines,
telling myself, like him, that I assumed them.

GAUGUIN'S CHAIR

Always in the love that men erect between each other
the nails and hacksaws are thrown away too late. From the remains,
legs, arms, back, seat—all puns—we raise a resting place
jaundiced, choleric, the male shade for yellow,
the male answer: to salve a wound with colors running from a wound.
His chair is not a grave from which to resurrect
what insists on throbbing at angles of the frame,
pectorals, triceps, these shifts from foot to foot.
The lit candle and book appear to anchor it
but they, too, have been hurled down, enraged
and tremble to stomp off, to shake out crackling breaths,
igniting those evenings within the yellow house.
Here a shadow, there another: Gauguin, Gauguin,
your furies lick the cadmium, touching it up to dance like yours.
Burnished with green, they feed on green and never will sit down.

AUGUSTINE ROULIN: LA BERCEUSE

Attended, Madame's gaze positioning your calm
beyond the foreground, where the pigment falls away,
you are the baby and the cradle rocked.
Her eyes that lock yours in a stout embrace
have chosen mottled greens for the full skirt,
highlighting the addition of the years
to a squat frame, the tunic's darker green
swelling her arms and shoulders. Why be ashamed,
the gaze asks, to admit I am not beautiful?
You have no poem to answer. The face is so composed
in planes which counterpoint the woman Van Gogh always sought
that orange light burning from within it glows
monotonous, munificent. By this last light you went to sleep
years past. And spent the years since seeking it.

GARDEN OF THE HOSPITAL AT ARLES

Bird's eye at first, your vision plummets down
until you cruise, flattening the foreground's trees
which stagger, fruitless, between two leafless elms.
Chartreuse beneath you, the little paths converge
at a pool of clear blue. The sky reflects in it,
all the sky you will see during this visit.
Four orange carp refresh by their insignificance
the oracular, suspended.
                    But you are still in flight,
born to take wing here and suffer wounded vision
that this garden be seen as Vincent would insist.
And so the agony must in part be summarized.
After the pond, the paths radiate again,
ending at another elm, more spectral than the rest,
a blue roofed shed, a stolid cook or maid.
And then the walls begin which enclose you on all sides
and rise to give birth to figures of the air
cramming the galleries, looking down on nothing there
and stairs which ascend to further galleries
more ghostly, of nothing but mauve light.
I told you there was no sky. There is neither day nor night
but that hour before seizure when the landscape waits, its breath
sick onto itself, when the yellow gravitates
to take hold of green and no stone will stand still.
Nights you are Vincent you wake to yourself like this.

III

IRISES

Without your asking, certain prayers will open for you
in the morning light. They intend to be profuse.
So, like the hush folded into these green wings
huddling the faces of the irises
which exchange their radiance with each other,
the answers will be countless, wordless,
as your appeals last night.
                              Can it be,
you ask, your solace while you stare
is no more than this choir of clear, blue fire
the heat has risen from so that angels can break forth
in jubilant cold flame?
                              In the asylum at St. Rémy
Vincent put down these flowers to stem the flood,
to keep the demons from himself while he kept watch.
And as he painted the waters parted that he walk,
that he believed he walked. While he burned there he believed.

MEADOW WITH BUTTERFLIES

If I could find asylum in flight
I would ride out on a wing glinting textures of the sun
passing through grasses where morning stalks the wild
down stamen and pistil, the indivisibles dividing up.

My name would be legion, my only voice the wind
settling my fluttering on anemone and pussywillow,
settling on dust in the gold calyx of sex,
and after sex, death's colder shallows, golder.

And when the fields received me, finally
down their thatched, darkling patches
high summer, I would cast off the encumbrance of the soul
and sink, all body, into a rich, burgeoning loam.

And you, to see me, would have only to repeat this.

ROAD WITH MEN WALKING, CARRIAGE, CYPRESS, STAR AND CRESCENT MOON

Wind that raises us that it reduce us,
lead me beside the still, unquiet current
in which Vincent has set the moon and sun,
female and male, pulsing, divided
from their rushes of light which seek each other,
divided them by one huge cypress, Father to all.
The tree sways in your rivulets of air,
dividing, Wind, the landscape, field and road,
the road engorged and fecund as the wheat.
In the midst of these enormous appetites
the tree warns us we must root in place.
Or walk between the tired workers bent toward home,
a spade over the shoulder, or visit an aged mother with our carriage.
Man or woman, we must find some work.
The earth is too much light to us, the sky too much.
Ravening is all. Wind, I must find some work.

THE ENCLOSED FIELD

So, this, too, is a happiness, whispers the man.
He has stepped into the field, the field is his,
cut off from the horizon by a wall
unscalable, cold purple. There an olive tree
squats atop the mountain, sentry to no one.
There the houses he will never enter
nestle the foothills in chill lavender.
The sun warms nothing, it is very ill
and cannot distinguish the morning from itself.
But in the field his body is all dancing;
he is a reed, a blue anemone,
his breath reddening each poppy, each breath slumberous,
never sleeping; he is the grass
parting to take the wind into its shaking
and bend it, break it, into song. He is this song
warbled to no one, chanted along the ground
where he will lie down, no one later on
but Vincent himself, Vincent among the fumes.
He will lie down with his demons in their flowering.

58

THE STARRY NIGHT

After that happiness, the contortions
wrung from their bodies and their words,
the woman fell asleep
while the man flew out to lose himself
in the language of a picture.
Oh, he knew how to turn
within the sinews within cypress boughs
spiraling above the blue hills' undulations.
He cast himself, another point brightening
beside the others, assembling, reassembling.
After he left his star, he settled on the moon
and bartered images for hours with Van Gogh
who from his nightwalk through the little village
soared up suddenly to trade illuminations.
Nothing they exchanged, though, could come to light
except what Vincent whispered should happen next:
before dawn I wake, the man inside the poem
facing the window looking on my yard.
Numberless above their reflection in the grass
the stars take off their crowns, I anoint them, they bow down,
dazzling from our infinite, appointed places.

PIETÀ

Of course, to die he had to bear a body
but once cold each Christ will rush down off the cross
and past The Virgin's arms.
Here, the flesh, pear-ripe, pliant to our glance,
repels her touch. She is a mother,
she will not insist her palm's open supplication
should hold him back. He is God, after all,
hurrying to meet himself again.
Behind all this, even as we watch,
the sky also plummets toward its conversion into evening,
the gold bleeding to cobalt suffering monotonous change.
Of course, especially around the eyes and sunken mouth
the spirit's lineaments too much resemble Vincent's,
though having read this in,
only another of the lost might try to keep him here.

PINE TREES

This, for those who notice, might be a crucifixion
which only to glance at undistracted
we could be driven mad.

Look, before the torment of the wind
drawing the crows across its yellow stare
like blood flecks in a yolk,

the pines have been nailed up, stripped.
Hacked off, the gashes raw,
gangrene widening their amputations,

they suffer us to call them less than human.
And the ground beneath them, mottled green,
divides its shadow, the light side stepping out

under a small rain's radiance, illumined.
Watch, the figure down right, her umbrella
that hue and texture of the rain exactly,

ambles away, her purpose to deflect you.
There is so much grief already
for all of us, she whispers much too loudly,

and those trees, we're all too old
to see what I saw, three of them and naked,
dead or not, we must not dwell on it

while she quickens her step across the miracle,
there's dinner to fix, my goodman will be starving,
raving if it's not steaming when he comes in . . .

as if in quickening she might leave the picture
or take from her shoulder the scarlet gash,
no doubt some accouterment of peasant dress

Vincent laid upon her to distract us.
While the wind, savoring the redolence of pine,
drops pine cones to prepare a resurrection,

dividing up our vision it stole blindly.

OLIVE ORCHARD

Through the window of his room he whispered down to them
and when they answered, Vincent drew up the trees
to divide the asylum's quiet, vigilant.
Inside, what dancing he awoke in trunk and bough
while one color responded to his thirst,
the thirst he tried to slake here, more invisible than white
circling with clouds outside at St. Rémy.
It was the absence of any shade he knew, this agony,
that begged the dizzy furrows the ground had raised to keep
swirling the bark chartreuse to blue and back,
asking the azure to answer leaf by leaf—
this color that he drank. He drained the cup.
It may have been of blood. Or wine. He may have prayed.
Outside the landscape slept in any case.

THE ROAD MENDERS

Cut off by the plane trees, the last extensions of their reach,
the sky, out of the picture, speaks for the unseen.
If a road be mended, I ask, can a man be?
I hear whispers among the boughs. The sky has answers.

First, the sky orders, you must attend to what is given:
the road, an upheaval, a pile of broken stone
mashed white, the sinews and ligaments exposing walks
a traveler like Vincent, repeating steps, broke up.

Note, the sky says, the black could be a graveyard like the sea
but the road has surrendered returning to itself
and so runs forward, a current charged by the huge trunks
it climbs and falls from, no end in sight, no end.

And still at the left, a goodman in a black hat
stoops to fuss at the smallest of the immaculate white blocks
on which he could be lettering, or re-lettering, or wiping something
    clean.
The sky insists: you cannot turn from this just yet.

Now it speaks from the branches, demanding that I catch
the absence of their leaves, the human body in the limbs
writhing, stripped naked. My legs begin to race in place.
The sky's voice breaks off. I turn, face the sallow yellow house

shuttered in green, the door crinkled like a leaf.
Two women approach, another freezes at the huge tree
clutching a bundle. All three are faceless, all three robed in black.
If there is a way through this, I can't see one.

Behind the trees I find myself, jogging the gold earth.
I pass stooped figures, golden, reflecting the gold ground.
The road is out of sight, the road runs in the foreground
miles from this dead center. I am right on someone's line,

a small target, the chosen one among so much bounty.
I look back through the gun's sight, see myself seeing myself,
the game safe until I will have earned my proper body.
This is the place the artist waits before oblivion or heaven.

PASSAGE AT THE ASYLUM

We are released, we stand
at the threshold looking in,
the word engorged in our throats
a password for the double door
at the end of the corridor
we never opened. We are free now,
we may speak of it without restraint.

The passage is a mouth, a cry
mottled in purple, yellowed
the hue of the new-born, the blue
tint of contusion.
When we arrived, we ran
the length of its arches, spiraling
backward, forward, to knock
at the doors on either hand
none of which open. At last
we resigned ourselves to the one
at the end, to prayer, gibberish.
We stripped words down naked
to whisper, obeisant, obedient.

But those who enter, like the redbeard,
enter raving, because the door
respects delirium and curses
even as it accepts, we thought,
our bended knee, our kiss.
Yes, we saw him go in
spuming. No, he never came back out.

And on the day they ran
in a procession down the purple,
down the blue and yellow festered,
the armed guards saluted
the door which had stayed bolted

and beckoned us to follow
jubliant in a throng.
Because the way we leaned together
like bread we broke together
took us into the world
speechless with happiness
to know the door was not for us.
And the words of the redbeard,
that one word, finally
was our wound, his,
the door had shown us
or a talisman against regret
vibrant in our throat
and when we spoke
no one but ourselves
might choke on it.

LANDSCAPE WITH PLOUGHED FIELDS

Never to be done running
down the furrows toward the stone wall
but always to be born back
that second his hand inhabits it—

never to finger the blue hills
without his wound inflamed, the blue wound,
without the scald sun his palm,
without begging for release, and then to run.

The man is a wind; he cannot cease
thirsting for earth to take him in
that he may claim a body can be his
and dance within the wheat and stand alone—

or blow as chaff, luminous over the field.
The man would turn to the thresher as he fell.

THE LAST SELF-PORTRAIT

Vincent, this is where our stars part company.
Your eyes here are taking down the thunderheads
flooding another shore, a point of vanishing
where the clouds break, the clouds break down finally.
Twice I have been there, I will not go back.
I snap shut the book of graven images
in which, time out of mind, your whitecaps wash you up.
With these words, brother, I set you straight beside myself.
Constellations swirl out of your jacket and your vest;
behind you a starry night breaks out, clarifies
dead stars swarming to life; look, golden, they explode.
Between them, Vincent, the shoreline of my own backyard
emerges, clouds lift, today is absolute and clear.
Friend, I am writing you this poem on that sky.

IV

PORTRAIT OF DR. GACHET

Mesdames, Messieurs, you who come to gawk
at this, my portrait, you idiots who lean
closer to tsk-tsk that these eyes are all tears—

remember: I catch your every pimple, hairs within it.
Weeping clears my vision. Inch up, inch in.
These eyes you see are mine, not his.

Everything else before you is Van Gogh:
my nose diagonal to the picture plane;
my frock coat's undulations churning up

into a storm, a blue squall's amassing clouds
shrouding this body; my background's calmer blue
sinuous, repeating Vincent's rhythm. Even the pumpkin

orange table supporting an elbow, a clenched fist
supporting a cocked head. Vincent, all Vincent.
Take me in, bastards, then question why I weep.

These artist eyes of mine, equal to his,
filled my house with paintings equal to his,
drew him exquisitely dead in his bed,

remember? You've seen it? A mere sketch—
equal to anything he did. Why, I fed him
laudanum we feasted on together,

toasted us with absinthe I needed for my nerves
more recherché than his. Under my roof nights
he never drank to one of my chefs-d'oeuvre

filling every wall but raved about his own!
Belladonna, morphine I would have ladled out
for one draught of praise to cross his lips . . .

Ah, together flying high on the white powders
from my closet—I thought those were our times,
myself the elect member of his circle—I was high,

tricked by exquisite nerves: Vincent was higher
on Vincent, Vincent nightshade, Vincent wine!
Look, in his hand a lily of the valley

from my garden unites us after death.
My eyes run over, catching its rich scent,
no, say it, they weep to see his paint

enshrouding me. No, I'm dead, I cannot weep,
I'm dead, I have no body but Van Gogh's.
Leer, stare, fools, I can pin you in a glance,

you I memorize in crying and despise
and keep here immortal in my eyes.
A hundred years of fools I've memorized.

UNDERGROWTH WITH TWO FIGURES

As if the sky had been conspiring
with earth to walk the earth,
the morning steps between them,
the birches process out of the mist.
And here they are: a woman and a man
emerging from one clearing to another,
stunned to take the forest in and still go on.
Look, the radiance laid along the trunks
is lilac flecked with gold and gold
cannot contain itself nor the lilies at their feet,
cannot contain the crocus, the wood violet—
nothing is enough, it rushes forth.
Watch, in the presence of such abundant light
fear burns off, all desire surrenders
to this one wish: that you and I assume their flesh
even as I speak it, that we relinquish
whatever colors stand for, whatever Vincent said,
in favor of our season's intimation
of a summer, of another after that—
this springtime of the bramble and the vine
we part continuing, this rank succession.

PEASANT GIRL

Promise me when you finish reading this
the girl will still be with you. Let her process
down the inelegant dull hours
in which the corridors of your day will lead you on,
the minutes windowless, circuitous, gray, peeling.
Promise that the wheat flecked red behind her head
may set the poppies throbbing here without forgetfulness,
that the wheat may continue, rising, gold
into more transparent leaf to match her hat,
her apron, that the colors may take your head and limbs
casting desire into another frame, shaping, breaking
each step you take. Promise she will still be here
when you are dumb, blind, stupified
with longing for her. And then in the figure of my light

promise you will read her again, promise again.

STAIRWAY AT AUVERS

Up, up the gold staircase the sun has run and faced
this goodman with a cane bent to his slow descent.
Then let him pass. So goes the sun's privilege,
to look on everything and take in nothing.

Here on earth the celebrants go forward two by two,
four ordinary women bowed in hope of an ascent.
And floating on the white billows lifting their common step,
the dirt before them widens, the dirt glints gold, glints green.

In dresses so billowing the bodies hide, untouched,
these ladies keep yearning wordless under their hats,
backs to us. And forever they will not show their common face
nor ever cease approaching the old man.

Of course, he is nothing. The stair is all to them.
If they could touch it, rub its gold down into their own,
lay that honeycombed coil against their skin, the pollen rising,
if they could remain as on this morning, setting out,

hoping to climb, to clamber, fall and scale—
if, if. What we see is a riddle on three stiff legs
descending, a face time has brought down
to one jagged line falling some other way.

This is how desire, evening and morning, crosses the body.

OLIVE TREES IN A MOUNTAIN LANDSCAPE

Vincent, all day the sky before rain outside my window
has rearranged one shape, a madonna and her child,
in imitation of your sky. Her ivory gown dissolves
against a darkling blue, the infant like a smoke
swirls and reforms with the mother moments later.
I am holding on. I think of your trees
as they come forward, some singly, some in pairs,
some trembling, arms uplifted toward my eyes.
They have come down from the mountain
that behind them, blue, denuded, rolls
like the fields, wave on wave, roiling their welcome,
in imitation of the gathering storm.
They have come down from the mountain
where eons have failed to make their vision good,
the peace they extended bough by bough
to whomever stood beside them in the cloud.
I am tired of your icons and your signs, brother.
I am holding on. The landscape you give me,
unpeopled except for what I read here of myself,
is all I see, processing on my window
whenever I look out. I read your olive trees
where there are none, and they are ancient, weeping now,
the harvest years back, they are in chorus as I write,
they believe I have called you out of death,
that a single word from me might save just one . . .
Today it will rain or not. I will go about my life,
resisting the temptation to read in a single shape,
opening myself to the sky under my feet,
to man, woman, child, my feet writing their own dance,
holding nothing as they go forward for the page.
By night I will be too spent to keep up any hope.
I will sleep the dead sleep only the living know.
Rest, Vincent, in the heaven paint made up for you at last.
There is nothing I learn from suffering but suffering.

SELF-PORTRAIT AS VAN GOGH

Before a mirror at midnight I compose myself,
donning the gold straw I tilt at just his angle
to assure the vision will stay caged.
I squint, ruffle my beard, henna the tips.

Or I bare my head, comb back the whorling locks
halfway to morning, tear all shades from the lamps
and rouge my cheeks, my pate, ruddy as the sun
turning the wheatfields in Arles to my vision.

Oh, the poses print can never flesh out!
The skullcap I snap on to play the bandaged ear,
hacking on a pipe, my throat inflamed . . .
The stupor assumed to lift an empty glass,
toasting the whores beaten off between my legs . . .
And then, at dawn, in my best suit, vest, gray bowler,
I stiffen to the pose of the finished gentleman,
the old disguise Vincent muffed until the end.
I sit down to breakfast sick. This is what they wrapped him in.

WHEATFIELDS UNDER A THREATENING SKY WITH CROWS

Last night I dreamed this poem. Alone in the field
I heard the wheat in answer to the wind
singing its response down golden stalk and chaff:
Vincent would come back, his risen body
a wing among these wings, which one I couldn't know.
I would find out at my death if I just asked.
At first I was comforted and happy to wait, mute,
while the sky poured over me a bevy of rich thunder.
But through this rolled the sun, purpled and gold
which prevented clouds' fruition as the rain.
The field held my feet rooted while I wept
that I was still in life, that Vincent lived in death.
I cried that I was finished with my words to him.

Today in the world the poems rain through my hands.
Go book, water the earth, they are repeating.